WASHOE COUNTY LIBRARY
3 1235 02848 5998
P9-DUX-715
DATE DUE

Sleigh Bells

and Snowflakes

A Celebration of Christmas

Compiled and illustrated by

Linda Bronson

Henry Holt and Company • New York

For my brother John,
"the Christmas kid"

A very special thanks to Teri Goldich and
the Dodd Center at the University of Connecticut

Henry Holt and Company, LLC
Publishers since 1866
115 West 18th Street, New York, New York 10011
www.henryholt.com

Library of Congress Cataloging-in-Publication Data
Sleigh bells and snowflakes: a celebration of Christmas / compiled and illustrated by Linda Bronson. p. cm.
Contents: Winter morning / Ogden Nash; We three kings of Orient are / John Henry Hopkins Jr.; Hark! the herald angels sing / Charles Wesley; O Christmas tree / German traditional; The friendly beasts / English traditional; Jolly old Saint Nicholas / American traditional; Jingle bells / James Pierpont; Long, long ago / author unknown; Silver bells / Jay Livingston and Ray Evans; How far is it to Bethlehem? / Frances A. Chesterton; Christmas everywhere / Phillips Brooks; Mister snow man / Bertha Wilcox Smith; Christmas legends / Denis A. McCarthy; Mary's lullaby / Ivy O. Eastwick; Christmas in the heart / author unknown; We wish you a merry Christmas / English traditional; O little town of Bethlehem / Phillips Brooks; Christmas prayer / Robert Louis Stevenson; Silent night / Joseph Mohr.
1. Christmas—Juvenile poetry. 2. Children's poetry, American. 3. Children's poetry, English. I. Bronson, Linda.
PS595.C48 S58 2002 811.008'0334—dc21 2001005438
ISBN 0-8050-6755-8 / First Edition—2002 / Book design by Donna Mark
Printed in the United States of America on acid-free paper. ∞

1 3 5 7 9 10 8 6 4 2

The artist used clay, collage, and paint to create the illustrations for this book.

Contents

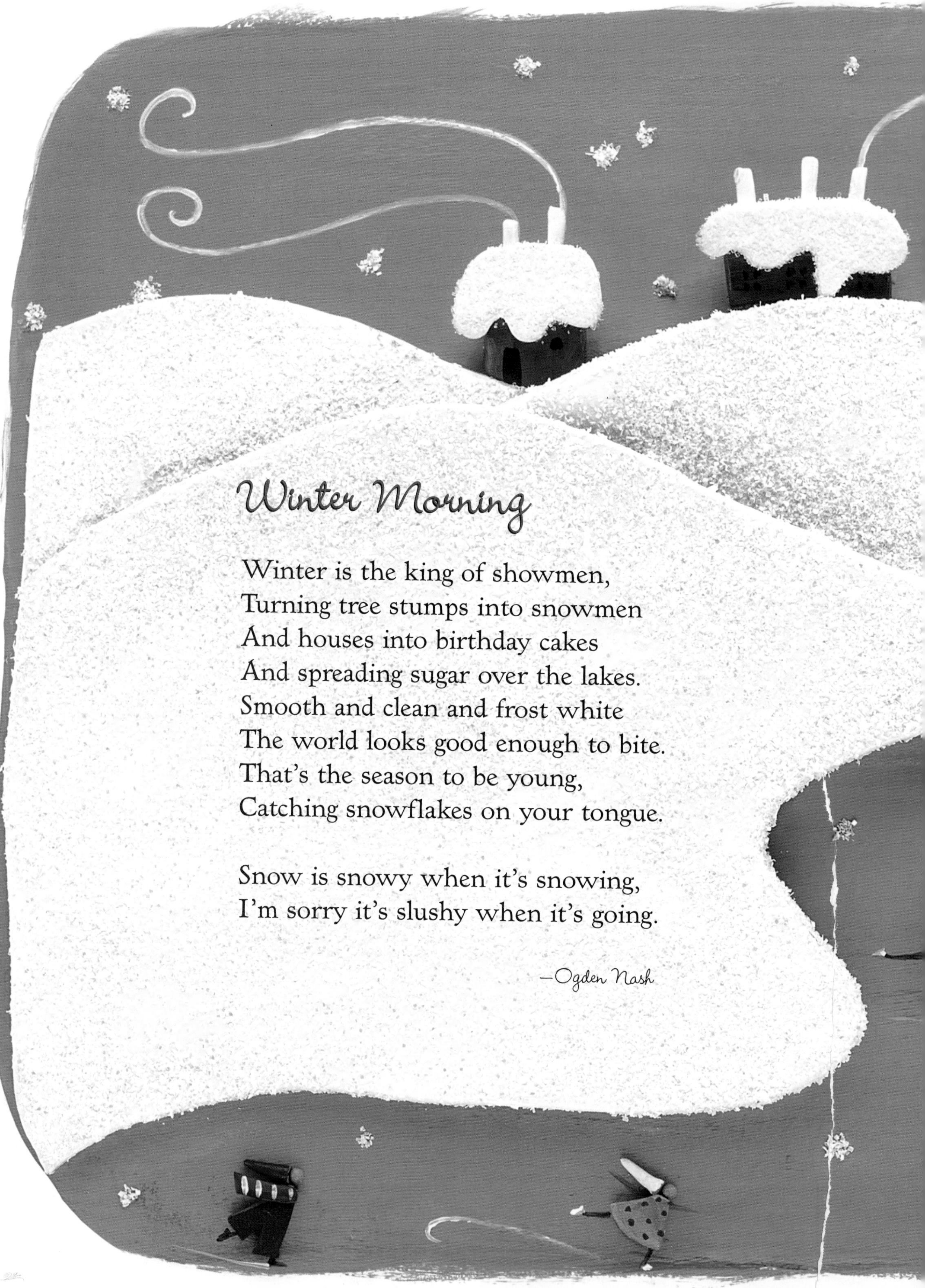

Winter Morning

Winter is the king of showmen,
Turning tree stumps into snowmen
And houses into birthday cakes
And spreading sugar over the lakes.
Smooth and clean and frost white
The world looks good enough to bite.
That's the season to be young,
Catching snowflakes on your tongue.

Snow is snowy when it's snowing,
I'm sorry it's slushy when it's going.

—Ogden Nash

We Three Kings of Orient Are

We three kings of Orient are,
Bearing gifts we traverse afar,
Field and fountain, moor and mountain,
Following yonder star.
O Star of wonder, Star of might,
Star with royal beauty bright,
Westward leading, still proceeding,
Guide us to thy perfect light.

—John Henry Hopkins, Jr.

Hark! the Herald Angels Sing

Hark! the herald angels sing,
"Glory to the newborn King,
Peace on earth, and mercy mild,
God and sinners reconciled."
Joyful, all ye nations, rise,
Join the triumph of the skies,
With th'angelic host proclaim,
"Christ is born in Bethlehem."
Hark! the herald angels sing,
"Glory to the newborn King."

—Charles Wesley

O Christmas Tree

O Christmas Tree, O Christmas Tree,
Your branches green delight us.
O Christmas Tree, O Christmas Tree,
Your branches green delight us.

They're green when summer days are bright,
They're green when winter snow is white.

O Christmas Tree, O Christmas Tree,
Your branches green delight us.

—German Traditional

The Friendly Beasts

Jesus, our brother, kind and good,
Was humbly born in a stable rude,
And the friendly beasts around Him stood,
Jesus, our brother, kind and good.

"I," said the donkey, shaggy and brown,
"I carried His Mother uphill and down,
"I carried her safely to Bethlehem town.
"I," said the donkey, shaggy and brown.

"I," said the cow, all white and red,
"I gave Him my manger for His bed,
"I gave Him my hay to pillow His head.
"I," said the cow, all white and red.

"I," said the sheep with curly horn,
"I gave Him my wool for His blanket warm.
"He wore my coat on Christmas morn.
"I," said the sheep with the curly horn.

"I," said the dove from the rafters high,
"I cooed Him to sleep that He should not cry.
"We cooed Him to sleep, my mate and I.
"I," said the dove from the rafters high.

Thus every beast by some good spell,
In the stable dark was glad to tell
Of the gift he gave Emmanuel,
The gift he gave Emmanuel.

—English Traditional

Jolly Old Saint Nicholas

Jolly old Saint Nicholas,
Lean your ear this way!
Don't you tell a single soul
What I'm going to say.
Christmas Eve is coming soon;
Now you dear old man,
Whisper what you'll bring to me;
Tell me if you can.

When the clock is striking twelve,
When I'm fast asleep,
Down the chimney broad and black,
With your pack you'll creep;
All the stockings you will find
Hanging in a row;
Mine will be the shortest one,
You'll be sure to know.

Johnny wants a pair of skates;
Suzy wants a sled;
Nellie wants a picture book—
Yellow, blue and red.
Now I think I'll leave to you
What to give the rest;
Choose for me, dear Santa Claus,
You will know the best.

—*American Traditional*

Jingle Bells

Dashing through the snow
In a one-horse open sleigh,
O'er the fields we go,
Laughing all the way.
Bells on bobtail ring,
Making spirits bright;
What fun it is to laugh and sing
A sleighing song tonight.

Jingle Bells! Jingle Bells!
Jingle all the way!
Oh, what fun it is to ride
In a one-horse open sleigh.
Jingle Bells! Jingle Bells!
Jingle all the way!
Oh, what fun it is to ride
In a one-horse open sleigh!

—James Pierpont

Long, Long Ago

Winds through the olive trees
Softly did blow,
Round little Bethlehem,
Long, long ago.

Sheep on the hillside lay
Whiter than snow,
Shepherds were watching them,
Long, long ago.

Then from the happy sky,
Angels bent low,
Singing their songs of joy,
Long, long ago.

For in a manger bed,
Cradled we know,
Christ came to Bethlehem,
Long, long ago.

—*Author Unknown*

Silver Bells

City sidewalks, busy sidewalks,
Dressed in holiday style,
In the air there's a feeling of Christmas.

Children laughing, people passing,
Meeting smile after smile,
And on every street corner you hear—

Silver bells, silver bells,
It's Christmastime in the city!
Ring-a-ling, hear them ring,
Soon it will be Christmas day!

Strings of streetlights,
Even stoplights,
Blink a bright red and green
As the shoppers rush home with their treasures.

Hear the snow crunch, see the kids bunch,
This is Santa's big scene,
And above all this bustle you hear—

Silver bells, silver bells,
It's Christmastime in the city!
Ring-a-ling, hear them ring,
Soon it will be Christmas day!

—Jay Livingston and Ray Evans

How Far Is It to Bethlehem?

How far is it to Bethlehem?
Not very far.
Shall we find the stable room
Lit by the star?

Can we see the little Child,
Is He within?
If we lift the wooden latch
May we go in?

May we stroke the creatures there,
Ox, ass, or sheep?
May we peer like them and see
Jesus asleep?

If we touch His tiny hand
Will He awake?
Will He know we've come so far
Just for His sake?

Great Kings have precious gifts,
And we have naught;
Little smiles and little tears
Are all we brought.

For all weary children
Mary must weep.
Here, on His bed of straw,
Sleep, children, sleep.

—*Frances A. Chesterton*

Christmas Everywhere

Everywhere, everywhere, Christmas tonight!
Christmas in the lands of the fir tree and pine,
Christmas in the lands of the palm tree and vine,
Christmas where snow peaks stand solemn and white,
Christmas where cornfields lie sunny and bright,
Everywhere, everywhere, Christmas tonight!

—Phillips Brooks

Mister Snow Man

A cranberry nose and a tin-can hat
Belong to a snow man, jolly and fat.
We rolled him up by the fence today.
Please, Mr. Sun, don't melt him away!

—Bertha Wilcox Smith

Christmas Legends

Christmas morn, the legends say,
Even the cattle kneel to pray,
Even the beasts of wood and field
Homage to Christ the Savior yield.

Horse and cow and woolly sheep
Wake themselves from their heavy sleep,
Bending heads and knees to Him
Who came to earth in a stable dim.

Far away in the forest dark
Creatures timidly wake and hark,
Feather bird and furry beast
Turn their eyes to the mystic East.

Loud at the dawning, chanticleer
Sounds his note, the rest of the year,
But Christmas Eve the whole night long
Honoring Christ he sings his song.

Christmas morn the legends say,
Even the cattle kneel to pray,
Even the wildest beast afar
Knows the light of the Savior's star.

—Denis A. McCarthy

Mary's Lullaby

Little Dove,
Little Darling,
Little Sparrow,
Little Starling,
Little Light,
Little Joy,
Little Treasure,
Little Boy.

—Ivy O. Eastwick

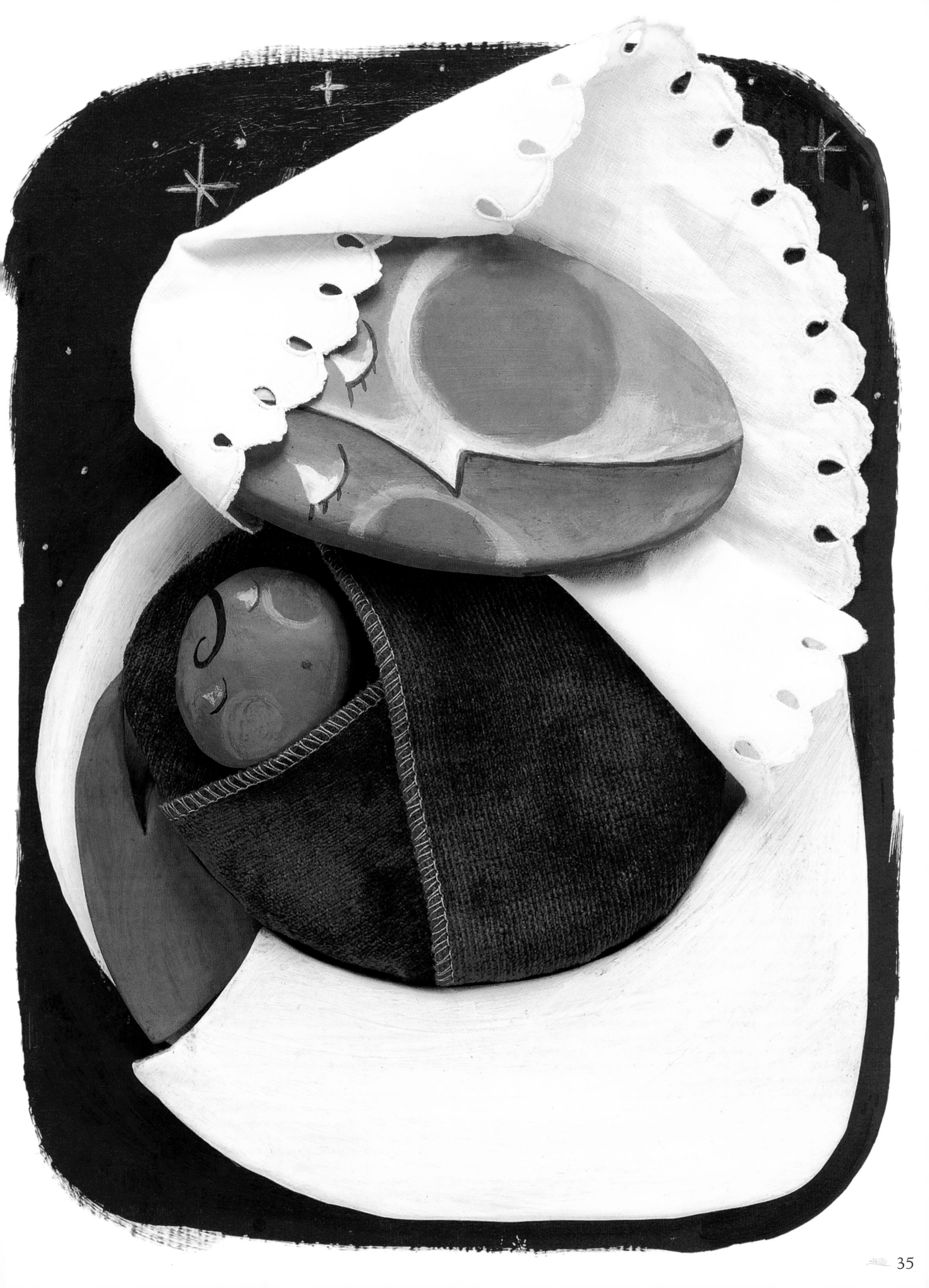

Christmas in the Heart

It is Christmas in the mansion,
Yule-log fires and silken frocks;
It is Christmas in the cottage,
Mother's filling little socks.

It is Christmas on the highway,
In the thronging, busy mart;
But the dearest, truest Christmas
Is the Christmas in the heart.

—Author Unknown

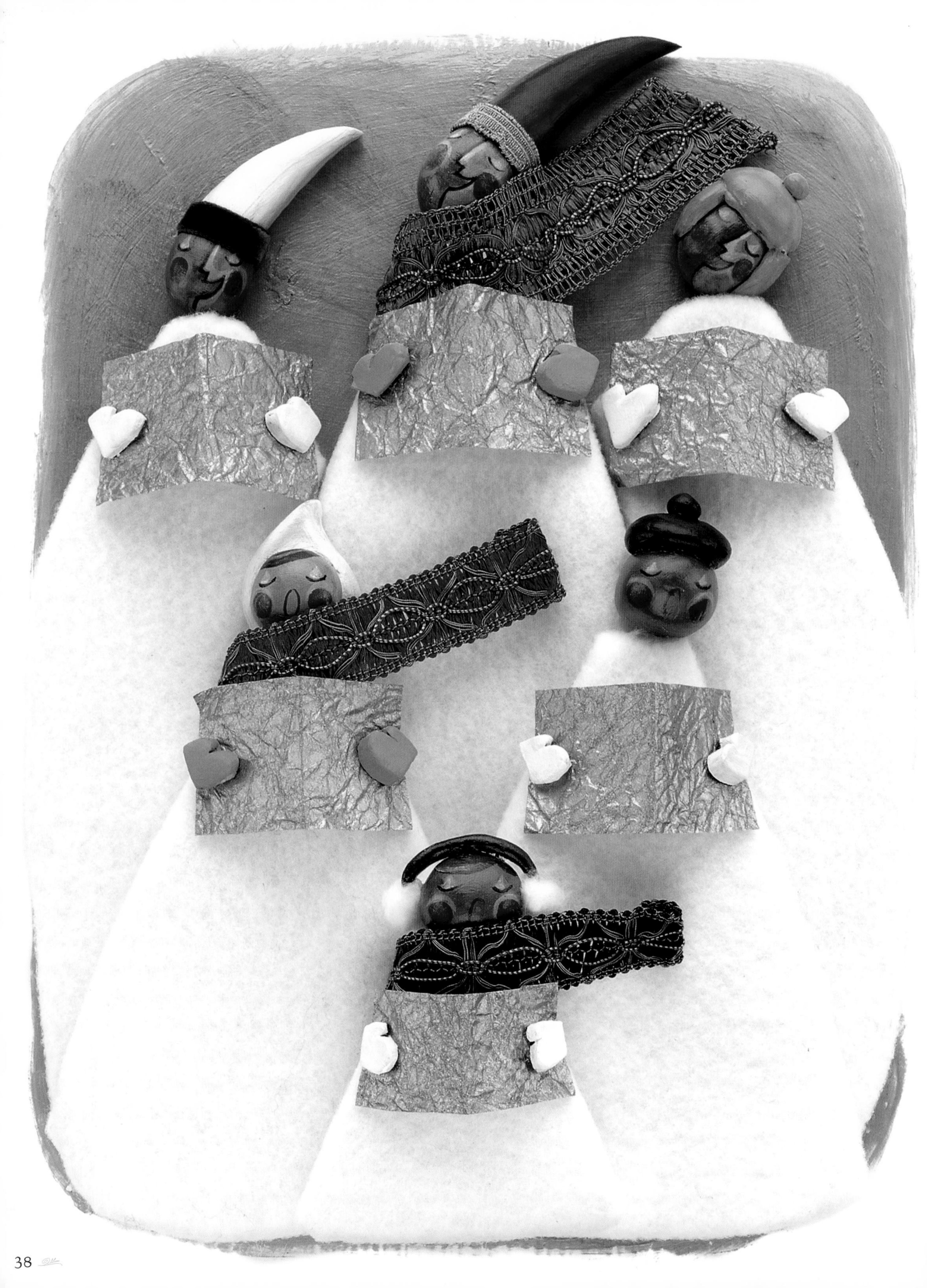

We Wish You a Merry Christmas

We wish you a Merry Christmas,
We wish you a Merry Christmas,
We wish you a Merry Christmas,
And a Happy New Year.

Good tidings we bring to you and your kin,
Good tidings for Christmas and a Happy New Year.

We wish you a Merry Christmas,
We wish you a Merry Christmas,
We wish you a Merry Christmas,
And a Happy New Year.

—English Traditional

O Little Town of Bethlehem

O little town of Bethlehem,
How still we see thee lie.
Above thy deep and dreamless sleep
The silent stars go by.
Yet in thy dark streets shineth
The everlasting Light;
The hopes and fears
Of all the years
Are met in thee tonight.

—Phillips Brooks

Christmas Prayer

God, our loving Father,
Help us remember the birth of Jesus,
That we may share in the song of the angels,
The gladness of the shepherds
And the wisdom of the wise men.

Close the door of hate
And open the door of love
All over the world.

Let kindness come with every gift
And good desires with every greeting.

Deliver us from evil
By the blessing which Christ brings,
And teach us to be merry with clear hearts.

May the Christmas morning
Make us happy to be Thy children
And the Christmas evening
Bring us to our beds with grateful thoughts,
Forgiving and forgiven,
For Jesus' sake. Amen.

—Robert Louis Stevenson

Silent Night

Silent night. Holy night.
All is calm, all is bright.
Round yon Virgin Mother and Child.
Holy Infant so tender and mild,
Sleep in heavenly peace,
Sleep in heavenly peace.

—Joseph Mohr